BMX

BY JOHN HAMILTON

A&D Xtreme
An imprint of Abdo Publishing | www.abdopublishing.com

Visit us at
www.abdopublishing.com

Published by Abdo Publishing Company, a division of ABDO, PO Box 398166, Minneapolis, Minnesota 55439. Copyright ©2015 by Abdo Consulting Group, Inc. International copyrights reserved in all countries. No part of this book may be reproduced in any form without written permission from the publisher. A&D Xtreme™ is a trademark and logo of Abdo Publishing Company.

Printed in the United States of America, North Mankato, Minnesota.
052014
092014

 PRINTED ON RECYCLED PAPER

Editor: Sue Hamilton
Graphic Design: John Hamilton
Cover Photo: Thinkstock
Interior Photos: Corbis, pg. 4-5, 8, 10, 11, 13, 14, 15 (top & bottom), 16-17, 19, 24-25, 25 (inset), 27, 28, 29; Getty Images, pg. 6, 7, 22, 23 (top); Thinkstock, pg. 1, 2-3, 9, 12, 18, 20, 21 (top & bottom), 23 (bottom left & right), 30-31, 32.

Websites
To learn more about Action Sports, visit booklinks.abdopublishing.com. These links are routinely monitored and updated to provide the most current information available.

Library of Congress Control Number: 2014932220

Cataloging-in-Publication Data

Hamilton, John.
 BMX / John Hamilton.
   p. cm. -- (Action sports)
Includes index.
ISBN 978-1-62403-439-8
1. Bicycle motocross--Juvenile literature.   I. Title.
796.6/2--dc23

2014932220

CONTENTS

BMX: RACING, FREESTYLE, AND MORE

BMX stands for bicycle motocross. Racers compete on twisty tracks with ramps, whoops, and gigantic berms. Freestylers have fun shredding at BMX parks, half-pipes, trails, or flatlands. BMX bikes may be small, but there is never a shortage of big thrills.

Xtreme Fact: BMX racing debuted as a medal sport at the 2008 Summer Olympic Games in Beijing, China.

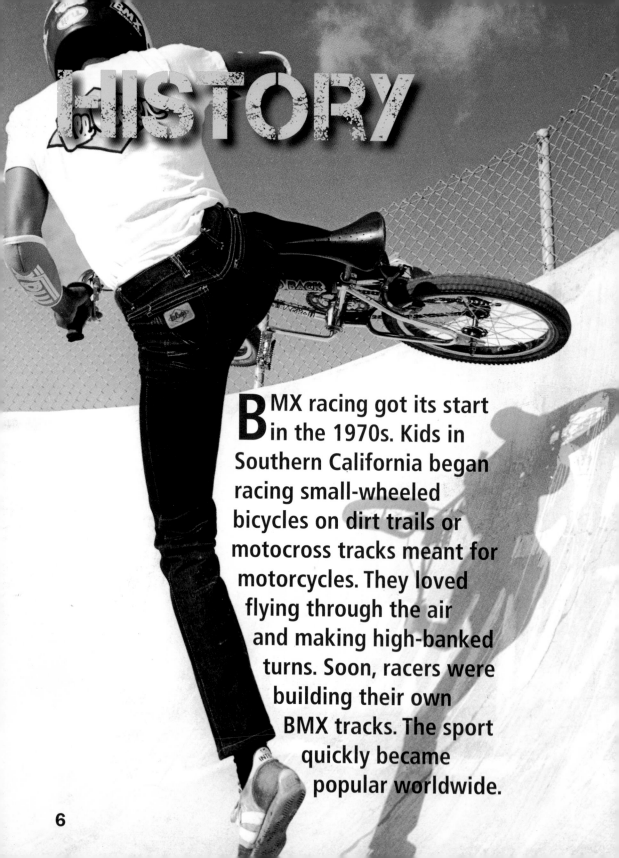

HISTORY

BMX racing got its start in the 1970s. Kids in Southern California began racing small-wheeled bicycles on dirt trails or motocross tracks meant for motorcycles. They loved flying through the air and making high-banked turns. Soon, racers were building their own BMX tracks. The sport quickly became popular worldwide.

Xtreme Fact: In 1963, Schwinn released the popular Sting-Ray bike (inset). Its small wheels made tricks easy to perform.

7

BMX BIKES

BMX bikes resemble mountain bikes with smaller wheels. They have a single gear. Their frames are made of steel or aluminum. They are strong and lightweight compared to normal street bikes. Wheels are 20 inches (51 cm) in diameter. The short distance between the center of the two wheels (the wheelbase) results in good handling on racetracks.

BMX racing competitors at the 2012 Summer Olympic Games in London, United Kingdom.

Wheelbase

Xtreme Fact: The short wheelbase (the distance between the front and rear wheels) makes tricks easier to perform.

SAFETY GEAR

Riding BMX bikes is a lot of fun, but head injuries and broken bones can occur. Smart riders always wear proper safety gear when racing or performing stunts.

Helmet
Also called a brain bucket, it protects both the head and face. Be sure to choose a helmet that is CPSC-certified (U.S. Consumer Product Safety Commission). Many riders also wear a face shield or goggles for eye protection.

Gloves
Good, tight-fitting gloves give protection, prevent blisters, and help keep hands from slipping off the handlebars.

Clothing
Serious BMX racers and freestylers wear long-sleeve shirts and long pants to protect their skin from cuts.

Pads
Top racers and freestylers always wear elbow and knee pads, sometimes hidden under their clothes. Top-quality pads use dense foam covered by high-impact plastic. Shin and ankle pads are also often worn.

Shoes
BMX riders wear tennis shoe-style footwear, with no open toes. The soles have good tread patterns to better grip the pedals.

BMX RACING BIKES

BMX racing bikes leave off accessories such as kickstands and reflectors. Omitting these extra items saves weight, which equals faster times around the track. Popular racing bikes include those made by Mongoose, Redline, Haro, and GT.

Pedals
Metal or high-impact plastic, with teeth on edges to grip shoes.

Chain
Racing bikes sometimes come with narrow chains that are 3/32-inches (.24-cm) wide.

Sprocket
Also known as a chainwheel or chainring. Racing BMX bikes often use a lightweight aluminum sprocket.

Crank Arms
Many race cranks are made of lightweight aluminum or carbon fiber, and come in two- or three-piece sets.

Sam Willoughby of Australia in action during the men's BMX quarterfinals at the 2012 Summer Olympic Games in London, United Kingdom.

Brakes
One handlebar pull-grip brake for the rear wheel only. Racing bikes use lightweight but powerful aluminum V-brakes. Front brake not needed for racing.

Frame
High-end bikes use lightweight aluminum or carbon fiber for faster racing.

Seat
Padded and adjustable up and down.

Wheels
Racing wheels are lightweight, with fewer spokes (often 28). Tires have deep knobs to grip dirt tracks.

13

BMX RACING

Each year, thousands of BMX racers compete on hundreds of hard-packed dirt tracks all over the world. Most racers are amateurs, but many are professionals who compete for money and prizes.

Nicholas Long (64) and David Herman (5) of the United States during the men's BMX quarterfinals at the 2012 Summer Olympic Games in London, United Kingdom.

No two BMX racetracks are alike. They range in length from about 900 feet (274 m) to 1,300 feet (396 m). Most tracks are well designed and groomed, with speed jumps, berms, and tabletops for exciting racing action.

Competitors race for the finish line at a women's BMX semifinal at the 2008 Summer Olympic Games in Beijing, China.

Competitors line up, or "stage," at a starting gate at the top of a steep hill. When the gate drops, the race begins. Starting in the lead gives racers a huge advantage.

The BMX course starting gate at the 2008 Summer Olympic Games in Beijing, China.

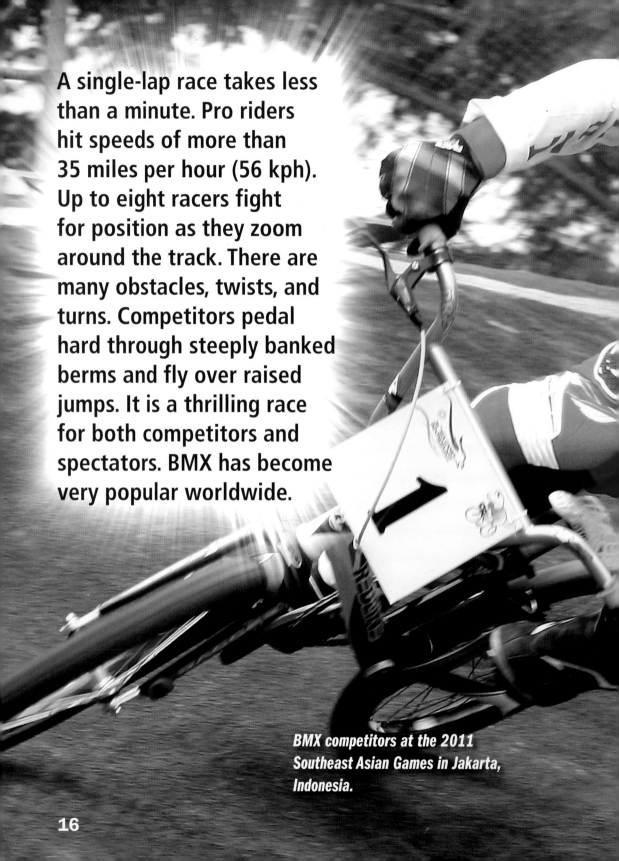

A single-lap race takes less than a minute. Pro riders hit speeds of more than 35 miles per hour (56 kph). Up to eight racers fight for position as they zoom around the track. There are many obstacles, twists, and turns. Competitors pedal hard through steeply banked berms and fly over raised jumps. It is a thrilling race for both competitors and spectators. BMX has become very popular worldwide.

BMX competitors at the 2011 Southeast Asian Games in Jakarta, Indonesia.

Xtreme Fact: In the United States, races are organized by the National Bicycle League (NBL) and the American Bicycle Association (ABA).

BMX FREESTYLE BIKES

BMX freestyle bikes are customized to do tricks on smooth surfaces such as parking lots, sidewalks, or skateparks. They are slightly heavier and more durable than BMX racing bikes. Top BMX freestyle bikes include those manufactured by Haro, Redline, Mongoose, and Mirra.

Pegs
Metal or plastic cylinders, screwed onto the wheel hubs, that allow for grinding, or sliding, the bike along ledges and rails. Riders also stand on pegs to perform certain tricks.

Seat
Often made of hard plastic. Riders sometimes stand on the seat while performing tricks.

Frame
Sturdy chromoly steel, durable enough for freestyle tricks. Pure flatland bikes have slightly smaller frames.

Brakes
Freestyle bikes have both front and rear brakes.

Gyro
Also called a detangler, a gyro keeps the rear brake cable from twisting when performing stunts that require the handlebars to spin around.

Tires
Designed to grip pavement, BMX freestyle bikes have smoother treads than racing bikes.

Crank Arms
Common cranks on freestyle BMX bikes are three-piece sets made of sturdy chromoly steel.

FREESTYLE BMX

Freestyle BMX began in the late 1970s when riders were seen performing stunts in skateparks or empty swimming pools in California. "Pulling tricks" soon became popular nationwide. World-class freestylers require nerve, countless hours of practice, and a sense of style and showmanship.

The best riders can perform dozens of colorfully named tricks. Some of the most popular include grinding, endo, manual, bar spin, wheelies, hang five, bunny hop, tail whip, tabletop, Superman, backflip, and Can Can.

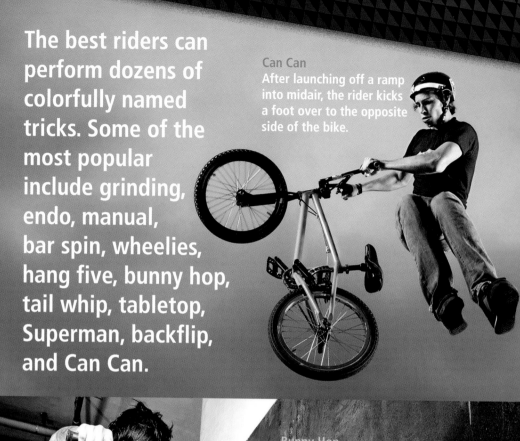

Can Can
After launching off a ramp into midair, the rider kicks a foot over to the opposite side of the bike.

Bunny Hop
Leaning back and pulling up on the handlebars while lifting the knees raises the bike off the ground.

FLATLAND FREESTYLE

Flatland freestylers perform stunts on smooth, level surfaces such as parking lots or basketball courts. Their BMX bikes are slightly smaller than other freestyle bikes.

Bar Spin
In midair, or with the front wheel popped up, the rider spins the handlebars completely around (360 degrees).

A shorter wheelbase makes it easier to perform spins and balancing tricks.

Endo
Applying the front brake and then balancing on the bike's front tire.

Manual
Balancing on the back wheel and moving forward for a long distance.

23

VERT FREESTYLE

Vert is a kind of BMX freestyle where riders use ramps to get "big air" and perform death-defying tricks. Ramps often include concrete or wooden half-pipes, quarter-pipes, or even empty swimming pools. A common vert ramp includes two tall quarter pipes set about 10 to 15 feet (3 to 4.6 m) apart.

A BMX vert freestyler gets big air at the 2013 X Games in Barcelona, Spain. Competition-level ramps can be 25 feet (7.6 m) tall or more. Riders launch off the ramps and perform tricks in midair.

DIRT-JUMPING BIKES

Dirt-jumping bikes are BMX-type bikes that share traits with their BMX racing and freestyle cousins. They are made to perform aerial stunts, but they are also built to handle the constant pounding of landing on dirt hills. Top dirt-jumping bikes include those made by Mirra, Haro, and Intense BMX.

Seat
Well cushioned to protect the rider from the shock of landing after a stunt.

Tires
Knobby tires with the heaviest treads for gripping the dirt track when launching a jump and after landing.

Shock Absorbers
To cushion the blow after a hard landing.

Brakes
Like BMX racing bikes, dirt jumpers have a single brake on the rear wheel, controlled by a pull-grip on the handlebar. Dirt jumpers usually use U-brakes, which are gentler than the V-brakes on racing bikes. U-brakes make it easier to perform some stunts.

Frame
Slightly longer than BMX racing bikes for added stability. More sturdy to handle the shock of landing.

DIRT JUMPING

Dirt jumpers like to ride on trails made of hard-packed dirt, with many ramps for performing stunts in midair. Ramps at competitions are usually bigger than on regular BMX racing courses, allowing riders to perform dazzling tricks. Ramps are usually built of dirt, although wood is sometimes used.

A dirt jumper competes at the 2013 O Marisquiño Vigo Urban Culture Event in Vigo, Spain.

Cameron White at the 2008 AST Playstation Pro action sports competition in Orlando, Florida.

GLOSSARY

Berm

A steeply banked turn found on BMX racetracks.

Brain Bucket

A slang term for a helmet, a vital piece of safety gear for BMX riders.

Grinding

When a BMX freestyler slides the bike's pegs across an object such as a metal handrail or concrete ledge.

Half-Pipe

A U-shaped ramp used for freestyle tricks.

Motocross

Motorcycle races that take place on dirt racetracks. Motocross is a combination of the French word *motocyclette* and the phrase "cross country."

Staging
When BMX racers line up at the starting gate. When the gate drops, the race begins.

Superman
A freestyle trick in which a rider comes off a ramp and then lifts both feet off the pedals and straightens his or her body parallel to the bike, as if flying like Superman.

Wheelbase
The distance between the center of the front and rear wheels of a vehicle. BMX bikes have a short wheelbase, which results in good handling and makes tricks easier to perform.

Whoops
A series of small hills or raised bumps found on BMX racetracks.

X Games
Extreme sporting events, such as BMX competitions, that are broadcast each year by the ESPN television network.

INDEX